FUN WITH MAGIC

Tricks and Stunts

Written and Illustrated by DAN NEVINS

WATERMILL PRESS

Printed in the United States of America. Watermill Press, Mahwah, N.J.
ISBN 0-89375-270-3

Introduction

Christopher Columbus once became angry when his friends laughed at his discovery of America. They said it wasn't such a great event and that anyone could have done it.

He showed them an egg and asked if anyone could stand the egg on its end. Of course, no one could do it. So he picked up the egg, crushed one end of it, and stood it on the table.

"That's not fair! Any one of us could have done that," they said.

"Yes, but none of you thought of it, and I did," laughed Columbus.

The magic tricks and stunts in this book are just like Columbus' egg. The problems seem difficult, but the solutions are always simple.

If you practice these tricks until you become good at doing them, you will keep your friends guessing for a long time! And you will always have the last laugh, just as Columbus did.

ESP

Tell your friends you have ESP.

You'll need a
box of crayons.

Close your eyes and
place your hands behind
your back.
Ask one of your friends
to take any crayon and
place it in your hand.
Make sure your friend
notices you are not
peeking.

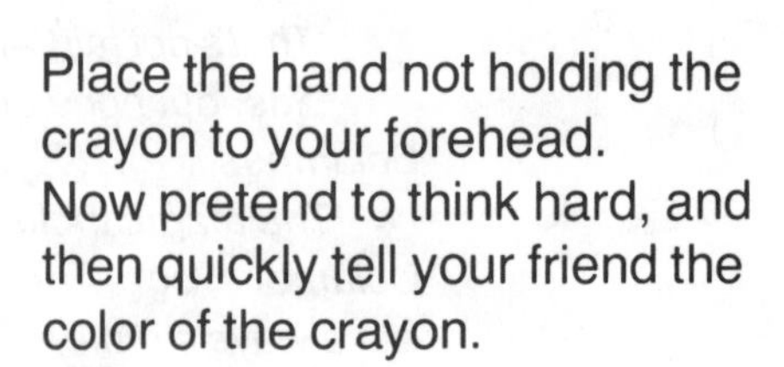

Place the hand not holding the
crayon to your forehead.
Now pretend to think hard, and
then quickly tell your friend the
color of the crayon.

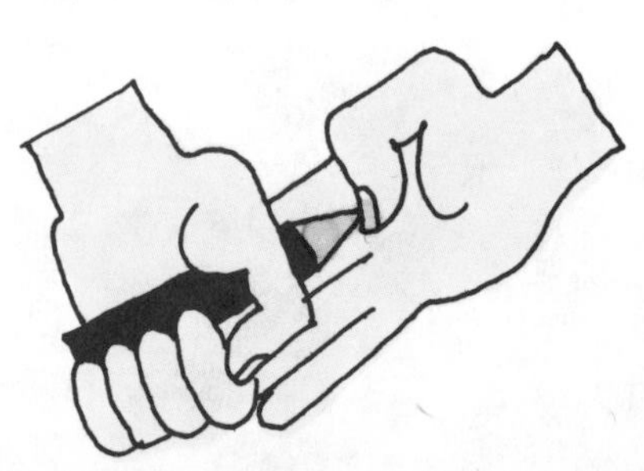

The trick is to mark the thumbnail
of your hand with the crayon.
You then bring your hand to your
forehead where you can see the
color.

Magic Paper Clip

Can you remove a paper clip from the bottom of a glass of water without getting your hands wet?

Toss a clip into a glass of water.

Make sure the clip is close to the side of the glass.

Now stand in front of the glass.
With your hand pointing to the bottom of the glass, slowly raise your hand.
The clip will rise!
When it gets to the top, pick it out with your other hand.

The trick is a small bar magnet.
Hold it in your hand like this.

Magnetic Hands

Do you know how to move mountains?
No? Well, neither do we.
However, here's how to move something small without touching it.

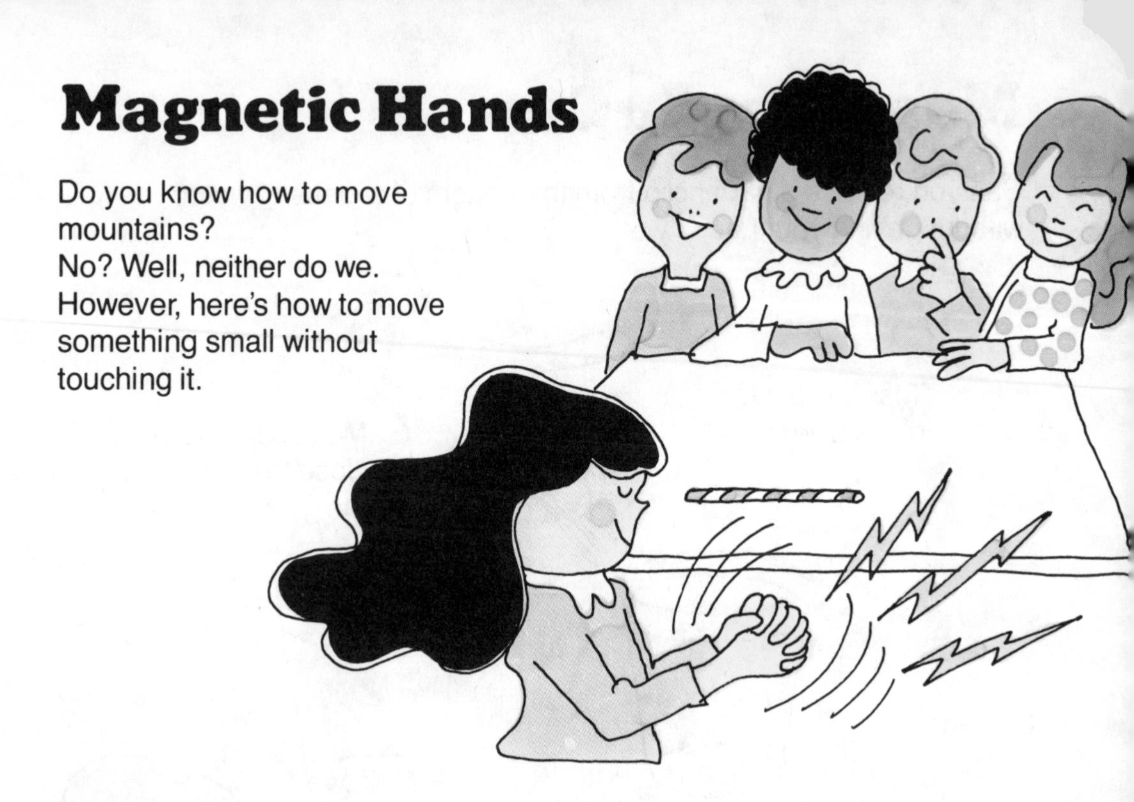

Place a straw near you on a table and have your friends stand on the other side.

Work up some "magnetism" by rubbing your hands together vigorously. Make sure your friends watch your hands.

Then bend over the table and quickly flick your fingers at the straw.
And while you're at it, *blow gently* on the table behind the straw. If your friends are watching your hands, they won't see you blowing the straw!

Steady Fingers

Tell your friends that you have the steadiest fingers in the world. To prove it, you'll need two Thomas Jefferson nickels.

Lay one nickel "heads up" on a table. Let each friend try to balance the other nickel on it. They will find it hard to do.

You can show them how to do it. Pick up both nickels and lay one "tails up" on the table. Proceed to balance the nickel on it.

The trick is to make sure you place the nickel *across* the two middle columns of the Monticello building. With a little practice it's easy to do.

Growing Inch by Inch

This is a neat trick, if you can do it.
Push a ruler up your left sleeve.

With a magical wave of your right hand, command it to come out slowly. Your friends' eyes will pop!

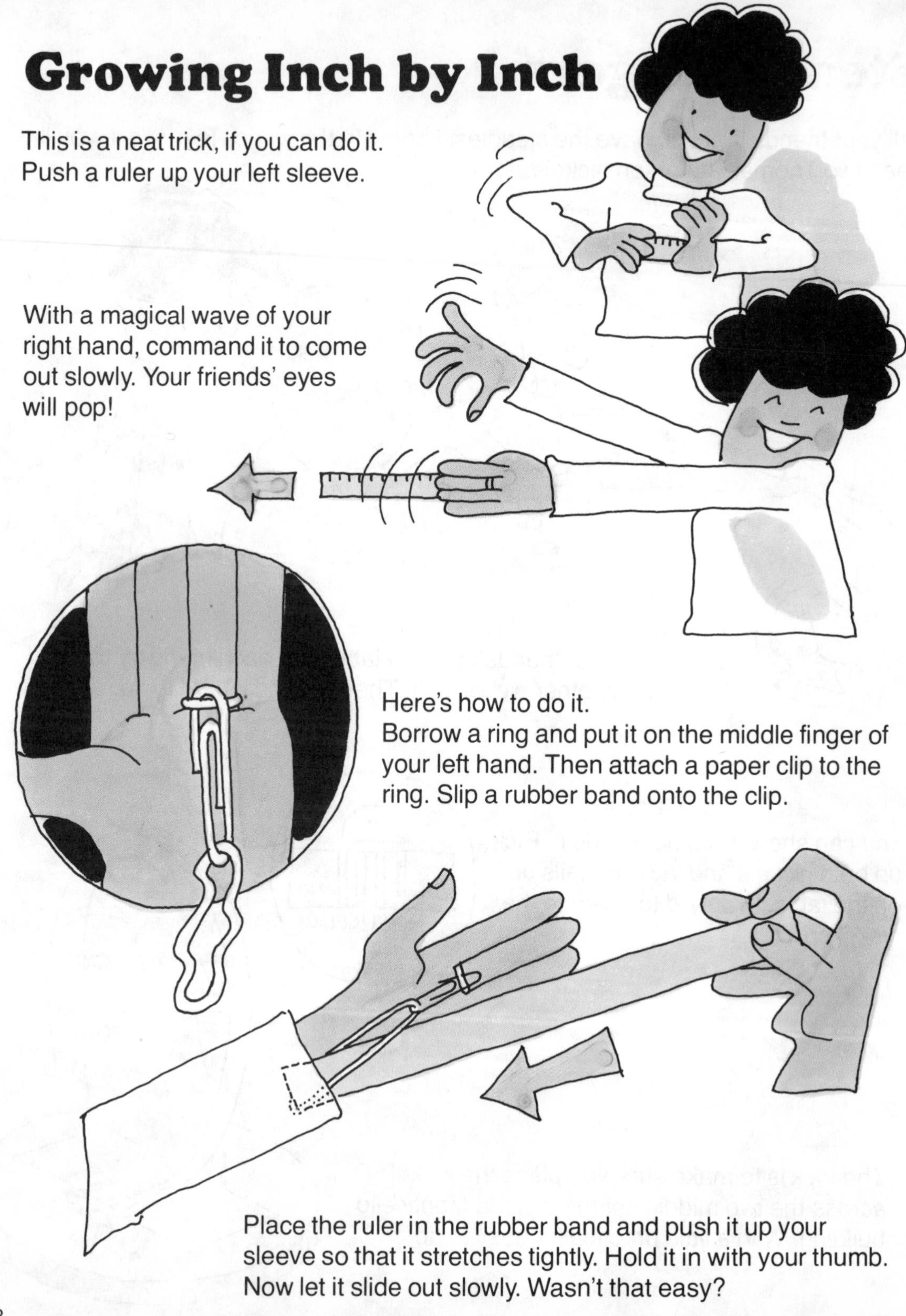

Here's how to do it.
Borrow a ring and put it on the middle finger of your left hand. Then attach a paper clip to the ring. Slip a rubber band onto the clip.

Place the ruler in the rubber band and push it up your sleeve so that it stretches tightly. Hold it in with your thumb. Now let it slide out slowly. Wasn't that easy?

Heavy Water

Tell your friend that once you fill a glass with water, he won't be able to lift the glass. He won't believe it.

Hold a book in one hand. Fill a glass halfway with water. Place the glass on the book near your thumb. Make sure your forefinger is free but out of sight under the book.

FOREFINGER

Cover the glass with a handkerchief and ask your friend to lift the glass. He'll do it easily.

Now remove the handkerchief and put a little more water into the glass. Cover it again and ask your friend to lift the glass once more. He'll find it impossible.

Under the handkerchief bring your free forefinger above the book, and hold the glass tightly with your two fingers. It's a neat trick.

The Great Seer

Can you make predictions? Tell your friends about it.

However, before they arrive, take a card from a deck of cards, and write its name on a piece of paper. Seal the paper inside a long envelope.

Now put the card underneath and along the edge of the envelope. Make sure the card *faces down.*

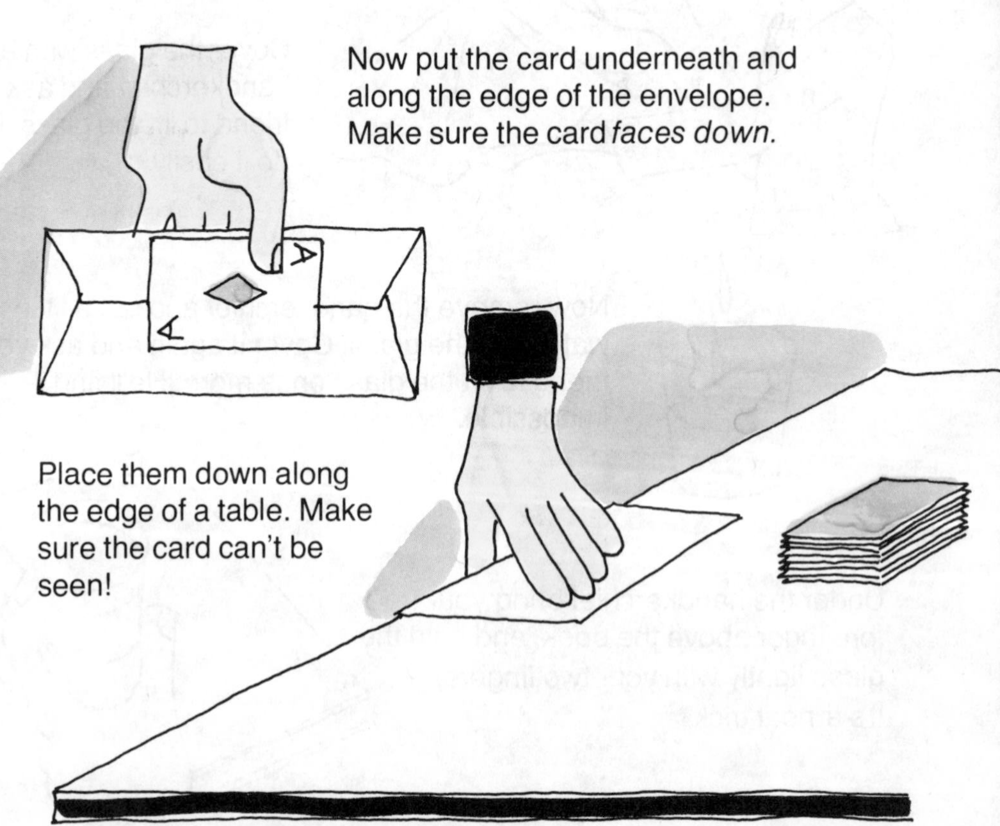

Place them down along the edge of a table. Make sure the card can't be seen!

When your friends arrive, have one of them shuffle the other cards and stack them *face down* on the table.

With a little swooning on your part, lift the envelope and card and place them directly on top of the pack.

Ask one friend to lift the envelope off the pack and open it up. When he has read the prediction, ask another friend to turn over the *top* card. Wow!

Banana Split

You will need a needle and thread, and a banana. Sew the thread through one corner of the banana, and out the second corner. Make a loop and bring the needle back into the same hole. Sew to the third corner. Again make a loop.

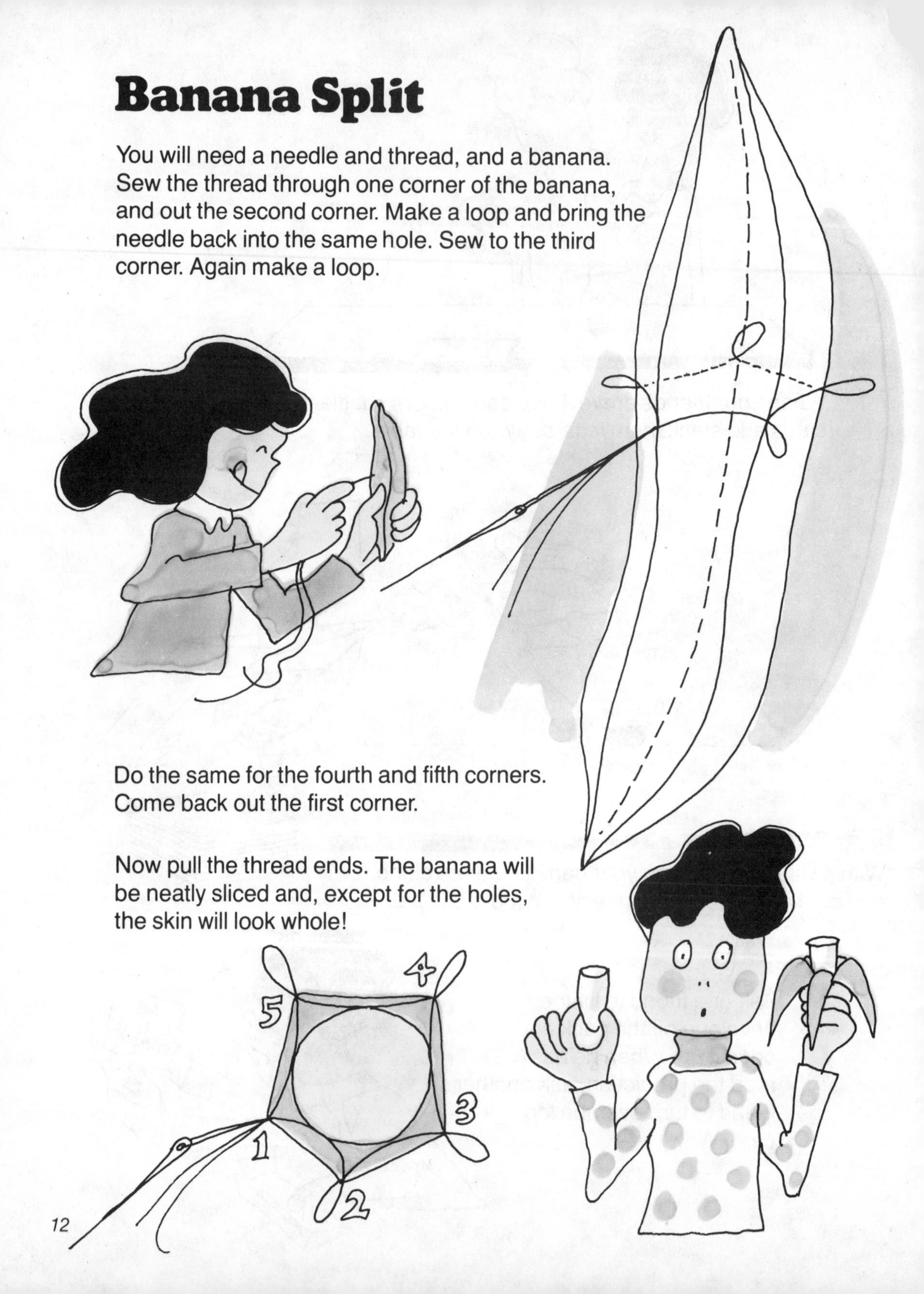

Do the same for the fourth and fifth corners. Come back out the first corner.

Now pull the thread ends. The banana will be neatly sliced and, except for the holes, the skin will look whole!

Human Vacuum Cleaner

Drop a piece of paper on the floor and ask your friends if they can pick it up with no hands.

Tell them you can do it with air alone.

Bend over and proceed to "suck" the paper off the floor with a straw.

Don't smile!

Disappearing Spot

This is a fun trick to do. Put a mark on your friend's hand. When you rub it off, she'll be surprised to find it on her other hand.

Before you begin this trick, touch the tip of your *left middle finger* in a dish of flour. Don't let your friend see you do it.

Now ask her to hold out her hands *palms down.*

Take hold of the hands and raise them a bit. Tell her they weren't the right height. At the same time *secretly* mark her right palm with your left middle finger.

Now let her hands go and ask her to wiggle one of her hands. If she wiggles the marked hand, tell her to make a fist and put it under her left armpit. If she wiggles the other hand, tell her you'll work with that one. *She must put her right hand under her left armpit.*

Use any excuse to get her to put her marked right hand under her left armpit.

Now turn over the left hand. This time let her see you touch the flour with your left middle finger. Then press it onto her open palm.

Stare at the spot for a while. Then quickly rub it off.

Tell her to open her right hand.
Shazam! There's the spot!

Look! No Knife!

Cut a cupcake clear through without a knife. All you need is a cupcake, a handkerchief, and a piece of strong white thread.

Place the cupcake on the corner of a table. Hide the thread under the handkerchief and place it beside the cupcake.

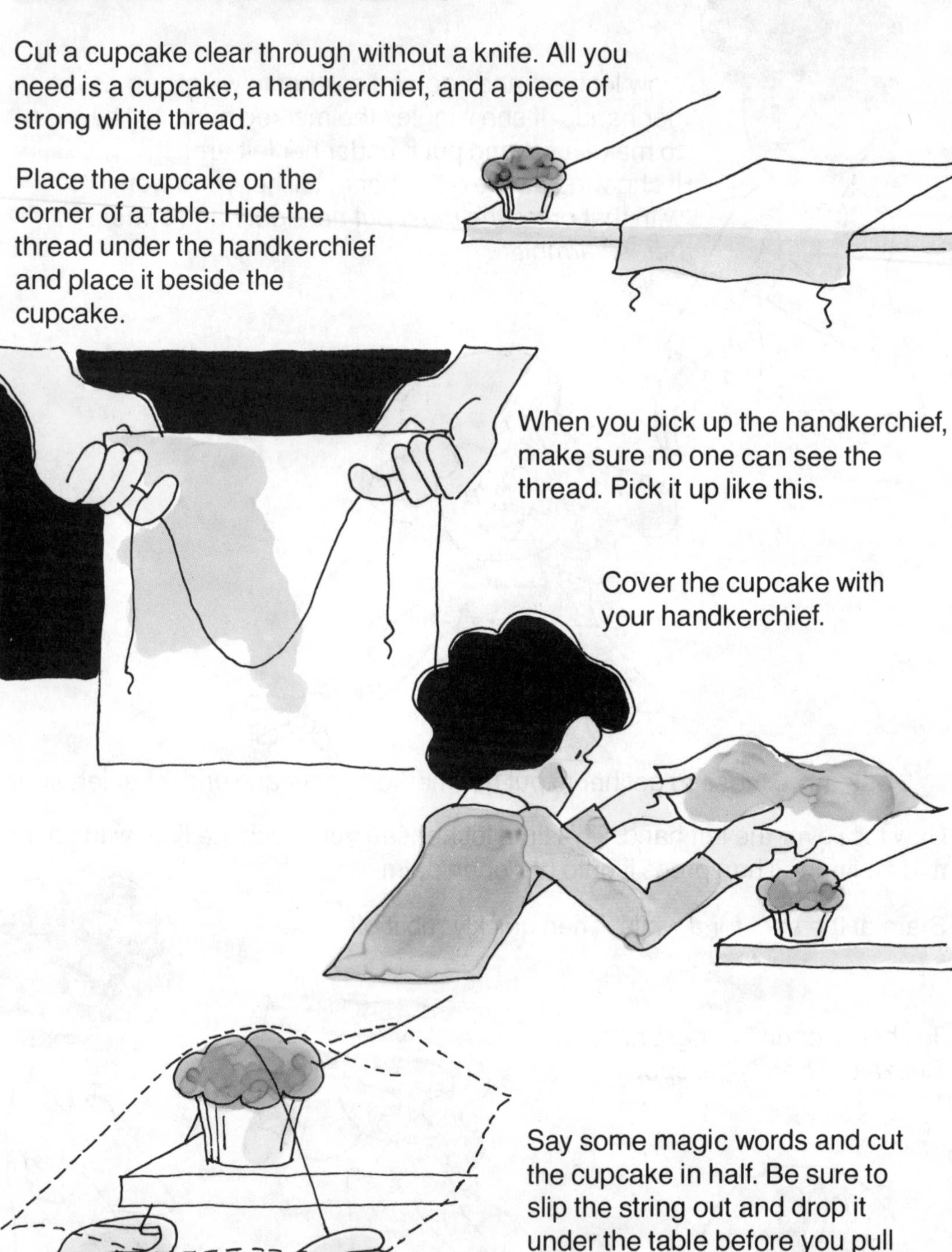

When you pick up the handkerchief, make sure no one can see the thread. Pick it up like this.

Cover the cupcake with your handkerchief.

Say some magic words and cut the cupcake in half. Be sure to slip the string out and drop it under the table before you pull off the handkerchief and astonish your friends.

The Numbers Game

Call a friend and tell her you have ESP and can pick out the name she is looking at in a telephone directory.

Ask her to take any number from 1 to 9 and add a zero on the end.

Reverse that answer and subtract it from the first number.

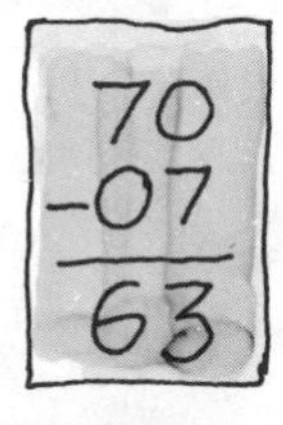

Reverse *that* answer and add it to the first number.

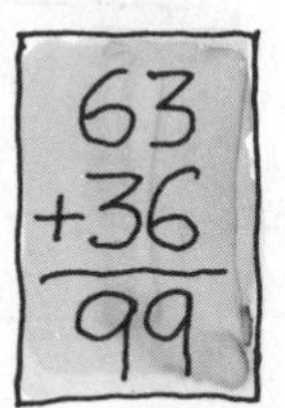

Tell her to take the last number (9) and turn to that page. Tell her to count 10 names down in the last column. Now you proceed to read off the name. Since *the answer is always 99,* you will have known the answer before you called her. Try page 99 too!

Shadows

You can make some delightful shadow pictures with the help of a flashlight or a lamp. See how many you can do.
It will help to make sounds, too!

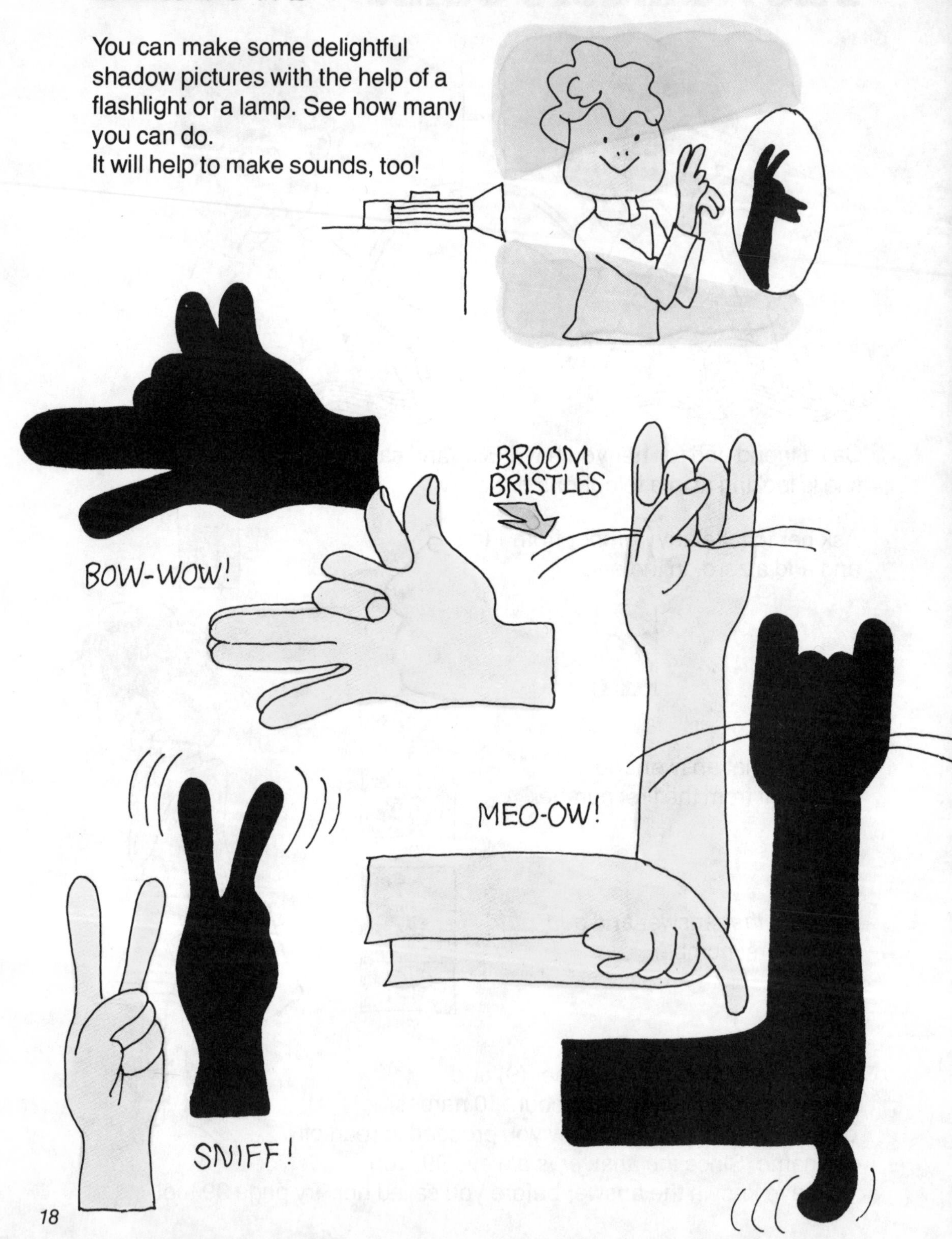

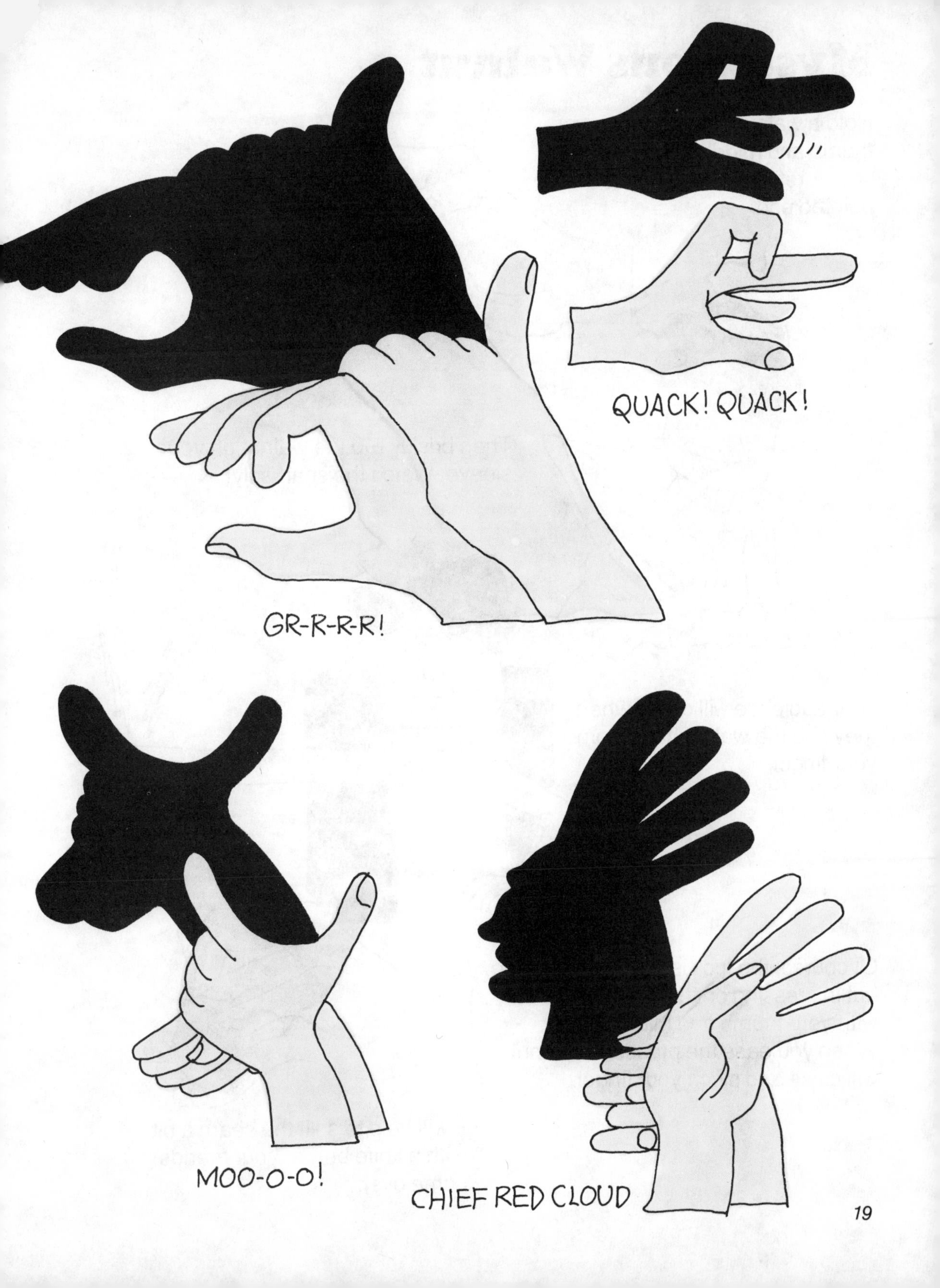
QUACK! QUACK!
GR-R-R-R!
MOO-O-O!
CHIEF RED CLOUD

Mysterious Walnut

Hold a walnut between your thumb and middle finger, with your forefinger touching the pointed end.

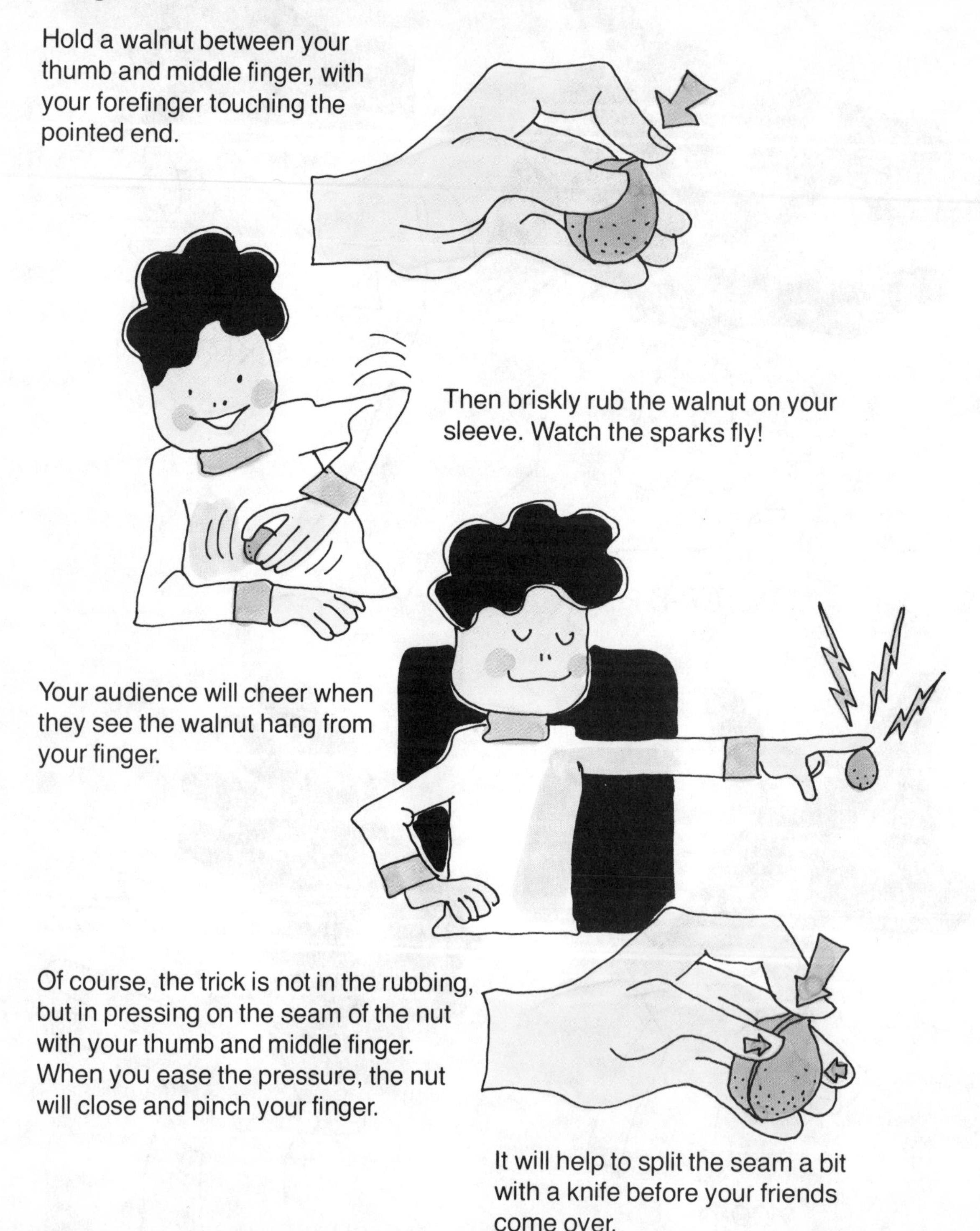

Then briskly rub the walnut on your sleeve. Watch the sparks fly!

Your audience will cheer when they see the walnut hang from your finger.

Of course, the trick is not in the rubbing, but in pressing on the seam of the nut with your thumb and middle finger. When you ease the pressure, the nut will close and pinch your finger.

It will help to split the seam a bit with a knife before your friends come over.

Juggler

Ask your friend to hold two dice outside of a plastic glass with his thumb and forefinger.

Challenge him to toss the dice into the glass one after the other.

The first one will be easy to catch.

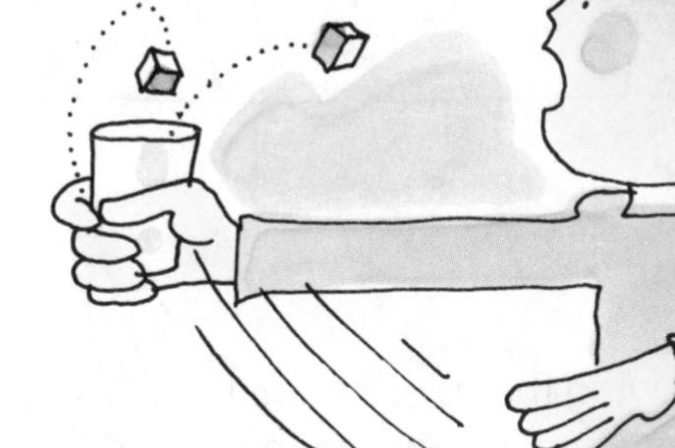

On the second move, he will catch the second die, but the first one will pop out.

Now show him how to do it.
After you toss the first one in, let the second die fall from your fingers. Then quickly *drop* your arm and catch the second die in the glass.

Ear Chimes

Hang a steel ruler about two feet long from a piece of string. Wind the string ends around each of your forefingers and then plug up your ears.

If you swing the ruler against an object, you'll hear the most beautiful bell sounds.

When they try it, they will be amazed at the beautiful sounds.

You can have a friend strike the metal against an object, too.

Cannon Booms

Here's a trick that will tickle your friend.

Have him put his hands over his ears. Then take a long piece of thin string and wind it around his head so that it runs across the middle of his hands. Pull the loose ends tightly and pluck one strand.

The sound will shock him.
He will imagine that he is listening to booming thunder or a roaring cannon.
Try it yourself.

Walk Through Paper!

When it comes to walking through a small piece of paper, you can do it. It's easy. Watch!

1. Take a seven-inch piece of paper and fold it in half. On the fold side, make six cuts about one inch apart. Don't cut all the way to the open side.

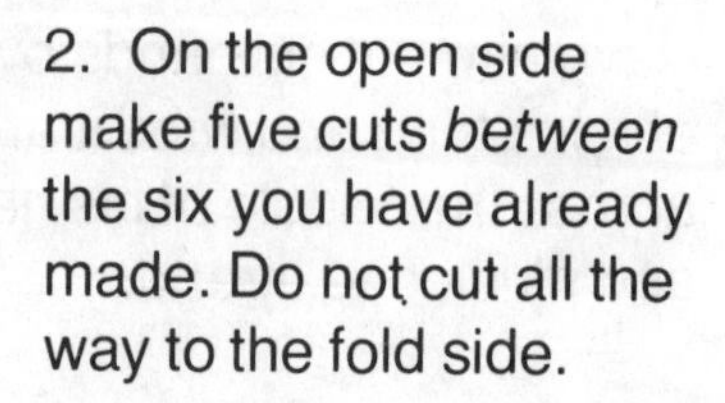

2. On the open side make five cuts *between* the six you have already made. Do not cut all the way to the fold side.

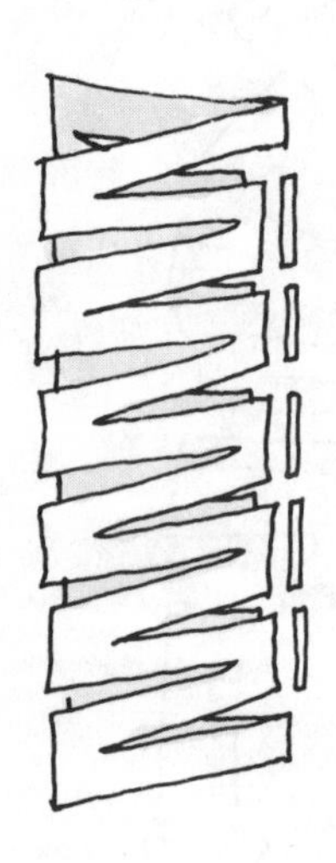

3. Then with your scissors, cut off the folded tips between the first and sixth cuts.

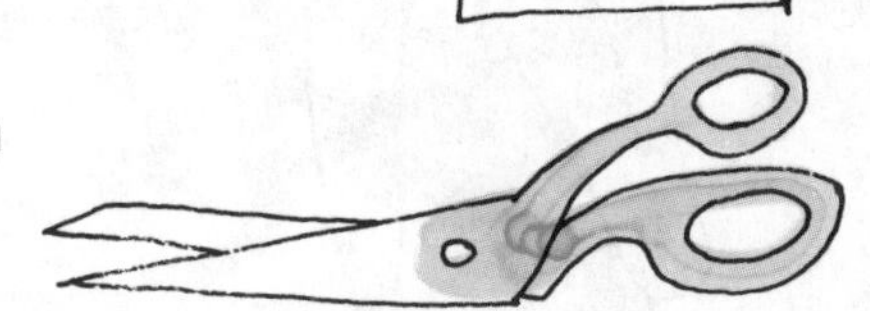

4. Now open it up and spread it apart. Your friends will be amazed at the hole. An elephant can walk through this paper!

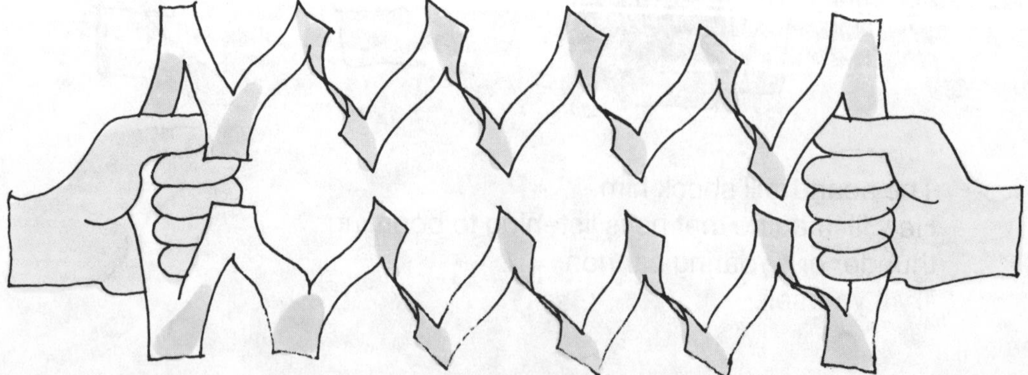

Penny Foolish

Make a penny disappear from a glass of water!

Show the penny in the glass to your friends and cover it with a cloth napkin.

Then have one friend take the glass and uncover it. Look into the glass. The penny's gone!

The penny is really in your palm. If you place the glass of water *on top of* the penny, it seems to be *in* the glass. Make sure you fold your hand quickly over the penny when he takes the glass.

Sailing! Sailing!

Tell your friends you can make an object float in the middle of a glass of water and that they can't.

You'll need a small juice glass, a small piece of aluminum foil, and some pennies.

Fill the glass to the top with water.

Now ask one person to place the aluminum foil in the middle of the glass and try to keep it there. Behold, it quickly floats to the side of the glass.

Let your other friends try their hand at it.
Each will fail, too!

Now show them how to do it.

Very carefully, place as many pennies as you need in the glass of water. You might have to drop three to five pennies, or more. But soon the aluminum raft will float to the middle. You've done it!

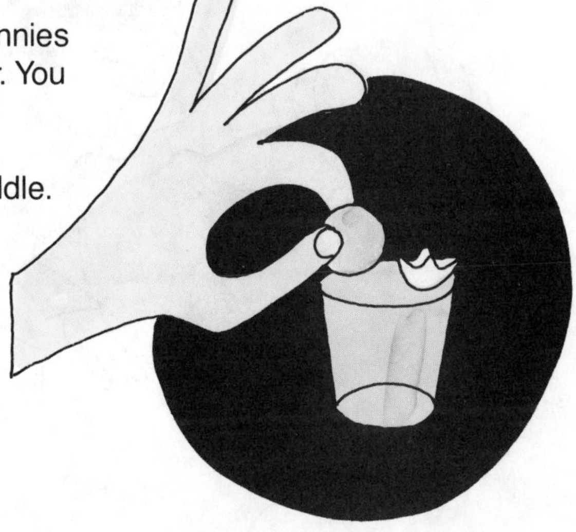

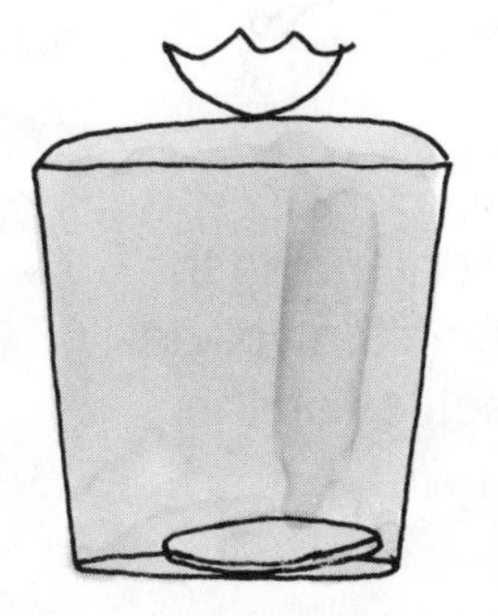

By the way, notice how high the water bulges above the glass rim.

Mixed-Up Egg

Do you know how to stand a raw egg on its end? No? Well, it's very easy.

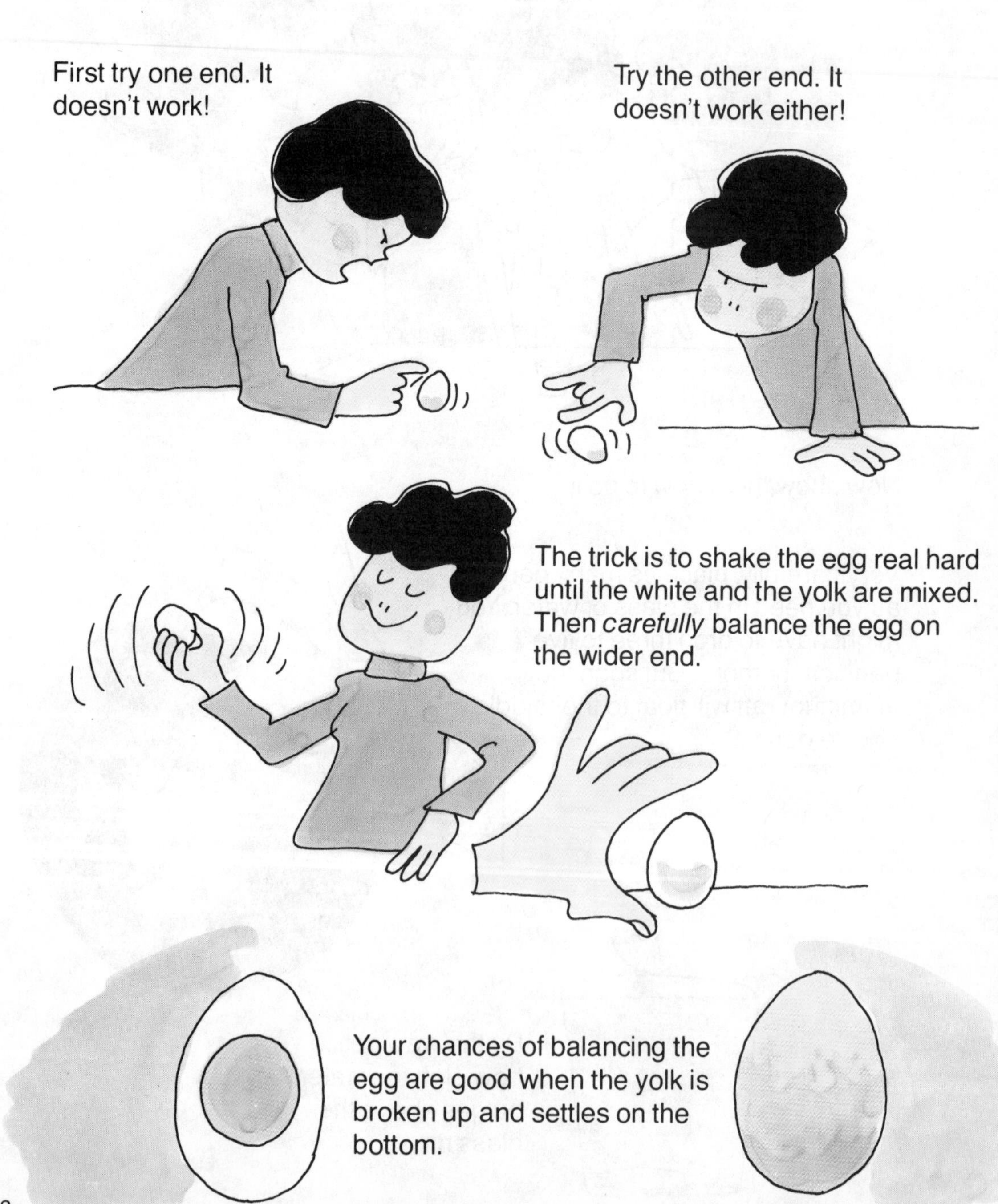

First try one end. It doesn't work!

Try the other end. It doesn't work either!

The trick is to shake the egg real hard until the white and the yolk are mixed. Then *carefully* balance the egg on the wider end.

Your chances of balancing the egg are good when the yolk is broken up and settles on the bottom.

Can Iron Float?

Yes, it can! You can do it by waxing a needle with a candle. However, that's doing it the hard way, and most of the time it won't work.

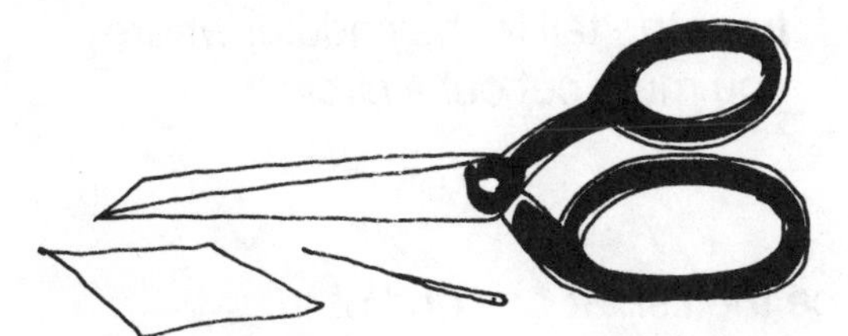

A surer way is to cut a piece of paper napkin and lay it on top of the water. Make sure the paper is longer than the needle. Then lay the needle on top of the paper.

The paper will sink after it is wet. If it doesn't sink, push it down with your finger. The needle will stay afloat.

Swimming Teacher

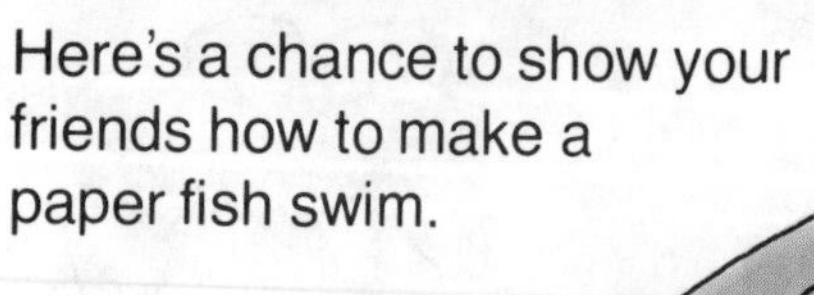

Here's a chance to show your friends how to make a paper fish swim.

First, cut out a fish from plain writing paper. Make it two inches long and color it to make it look real.

Then cut out a narrow channel from the tail to the middle, where you must cut out a circle.

Place the fish at one end of a shallow dish of water. Make sure the top of the paper fish stays dry!

Now squirt one drop of oil into the cut-out circle. Notice how the oil runs out the narrow channel and pushes the fish quickly across the water.

Ink to Oil

Here's a trick that will really make your friends furious. Tell them you can turn ink into oil!

Of course, they will laugh.

So, quickly pull out seven toothpicks and arrange them like this.

Before they can say "not fair," arrange the toothpicks to spell this.

You will have the last laugh.

Balloon Pincushion

Stick pins into a balloon.
Surprise! It won't pop.

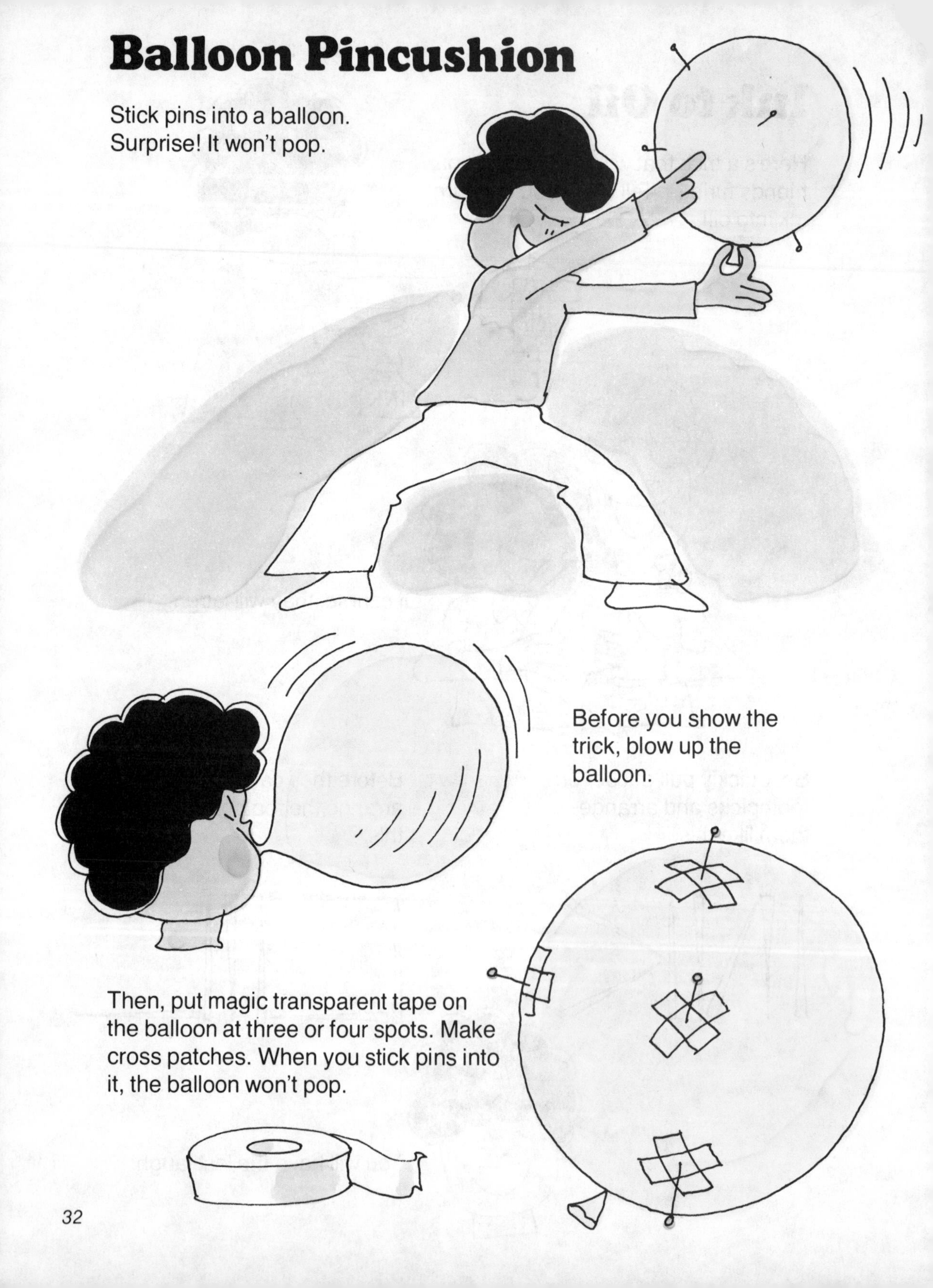

Before you show the trick, blow up the balloon.

Then, put magic transparent tape on the balloon at three or four spots. Make cross patches. When you stick pins into it, the balloon won't pop.

Bottle Show-Off

Tear a strip of tracing paper or newsprint about eight inches long and one inch wide. Lay it on top of an empty soda bottle. Then stack two quarters, a nickel, and a dime on top of that.

Now dare any of your friends to remove the paper without disturbing the coins.

After they have tried and failed, tear one end of the paper close to the coins. Then hold the other end straight out and hit the paper hard with your forefinger... the coins stay put!

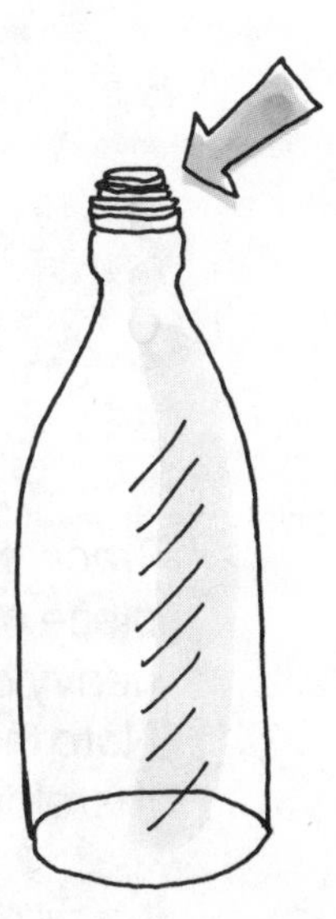

Boomerang

The Australian aborigine is an expert at throwing the boomerang. He rarely misses. We can make a miniature boomerang and see how it works.

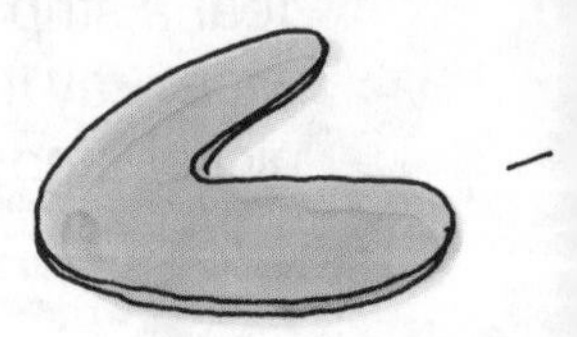

Trace the shape of this drawing on a piece of thin cardboard, or on a piece of heavy bond paper. Cut the shape out. Note that one side is fatter and therefore heavier than the other side.

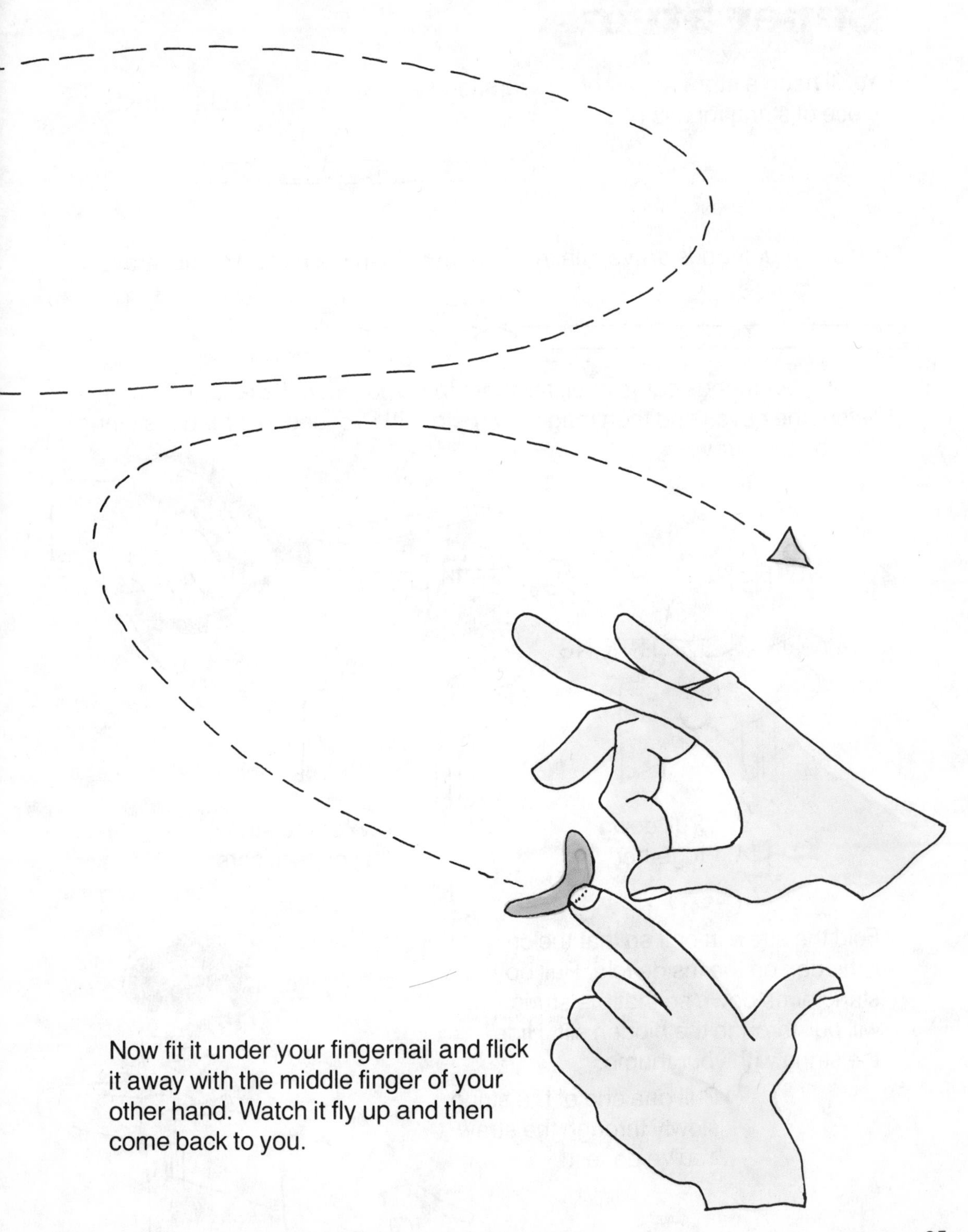

Now fit it under your fingernail and flick it away with the middle finger of your other hand. Watch it fly up and then come back to you.

Super String!

You'll need a straw, a pair of scissors, and a long piece of string for this one.

Before your friends arrive, make a two-inch slit in the middle of the straw.

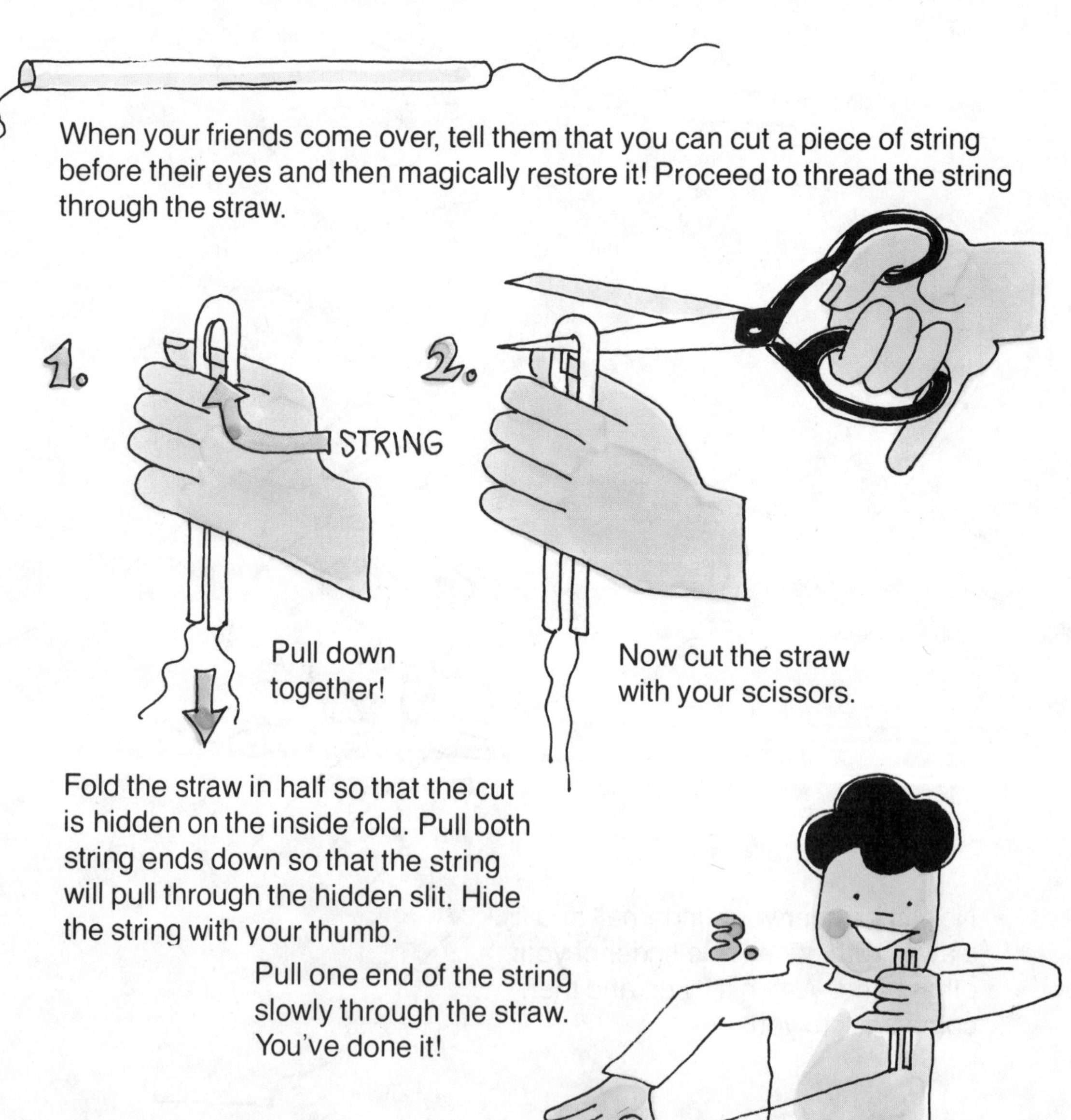

When your friends come over, tell them that you can cut a piece of string before their eyes and then magically restore it! Proceed to thread the string through the straw.

Pull down together!

Now cut the straw with your scissors.

Fold the straw in half so that the cut is hidden on the inside fold. Pull both string ends down so that the string will pull through the hidden slit. Hide the string with your thumb.

Pull one end of the string slowly through the straw. You've done it!

Balloon Bowling

Challenge a friend to a bowling contest with balloons. Tell her you can bowl a balloon farther than she can.

If you're smart you'll fill the balloon with sugar before she arrives.

Blow up your balloons and tie the ends.

Now bowl away! Your balloon will do the craziest wiggles, but you'll win. Your friend will be puzzled.

Halloween Witch

Halloween is a time to have fun with witches. See if you can turn your pumpkin into a witch like this.

Catch A Coin

Try this one.

Place a half dollar on your elbow and
try to catch it with one swing of your arm.
It will prove to be very difficult unless . . .

you *bend your knees* a little bit just as you
swing your arm.

Mighty Dollar

Show your friends how you can bend a straw with a folded dollar bill.

Fold the bill and hold it like this.

Have a friend hold the straw.

Now strike the straw. It's bent!

The secret?
When you're ready to strike the straw, stretch out your index finger. If you make a fast swing, your friends won't see the finger do the work.

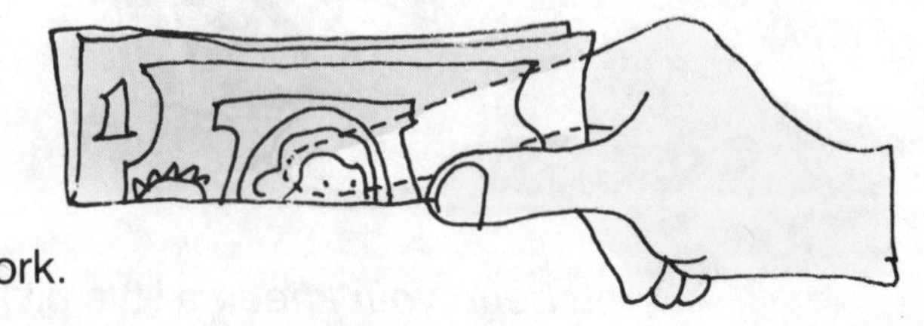

One-Sided Paper

Prove to your friends that you can cut a paper so that it has only *one side.* Your friends will say, "Impossible!"

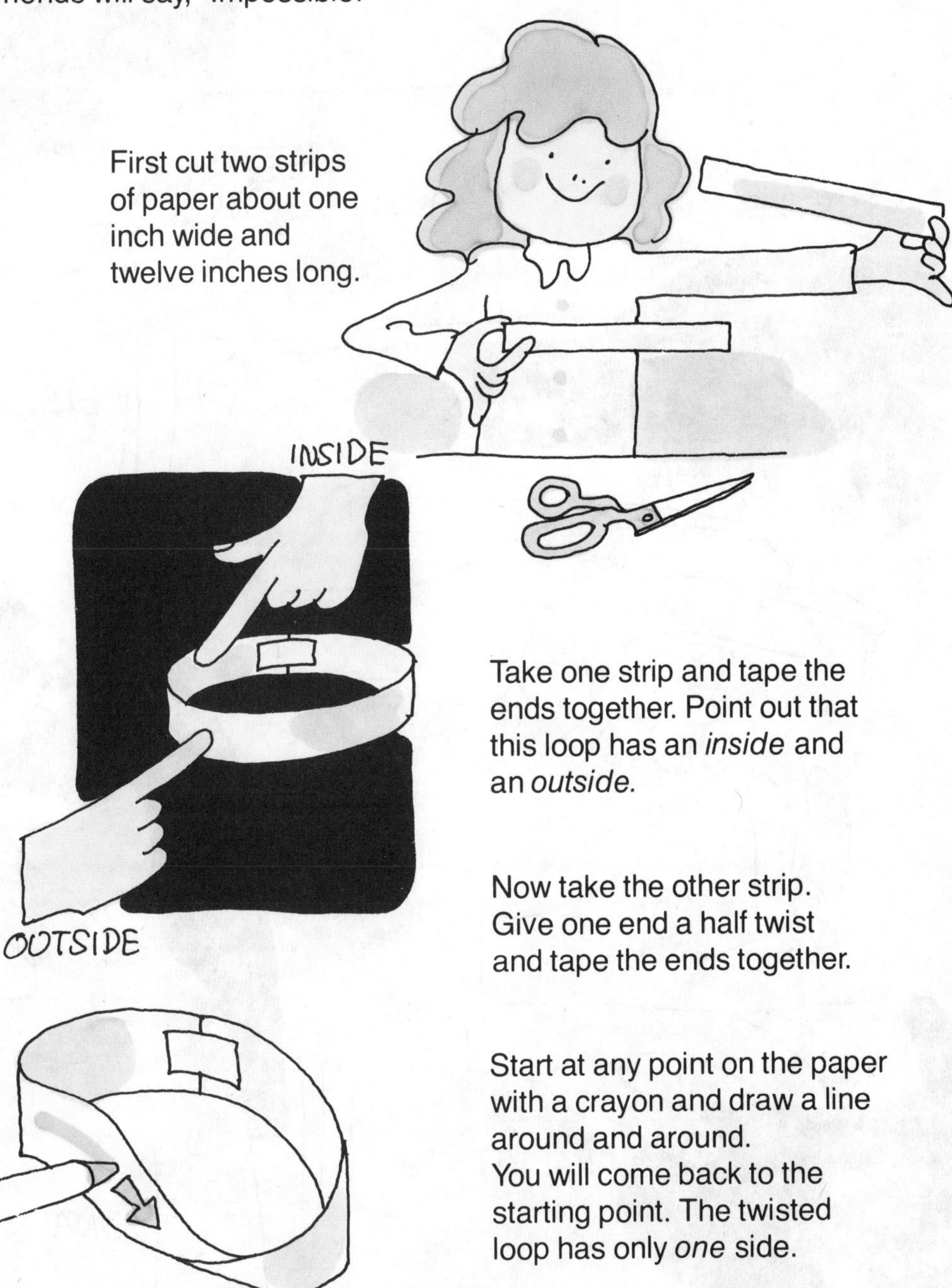

First cut two strips of paper about one inch wide and twelve inches long.

Take one strip and tape the ends together. Point out that this loop has an *inside* and an *outside.*

Now take the other strip. Give one end a half twist and tape the ends together.

Start at any point on the paper with a crayon and draw a line around and around.
You will come back to the starting point. The twisted loop has only *one* side.

More Shadows

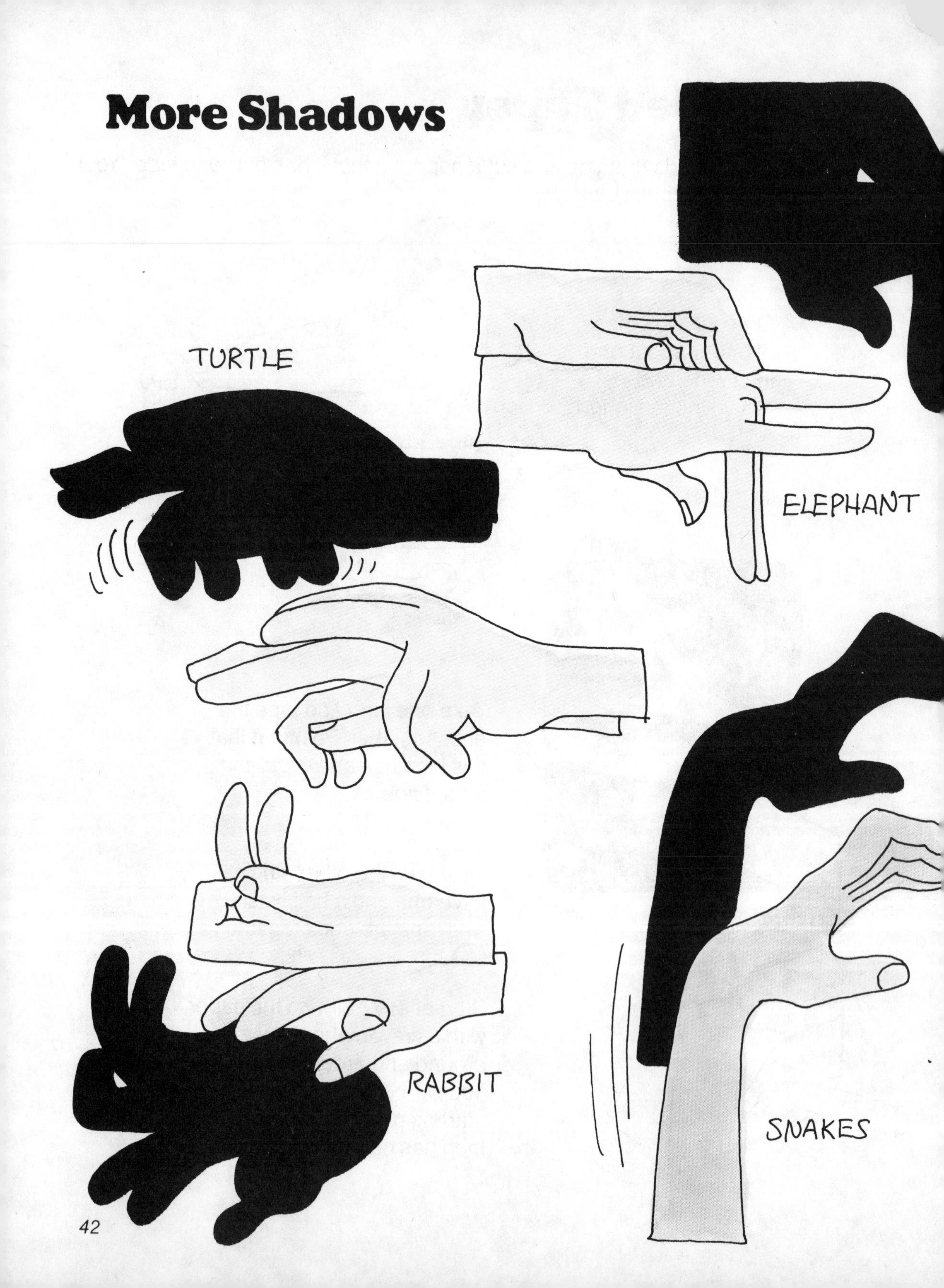

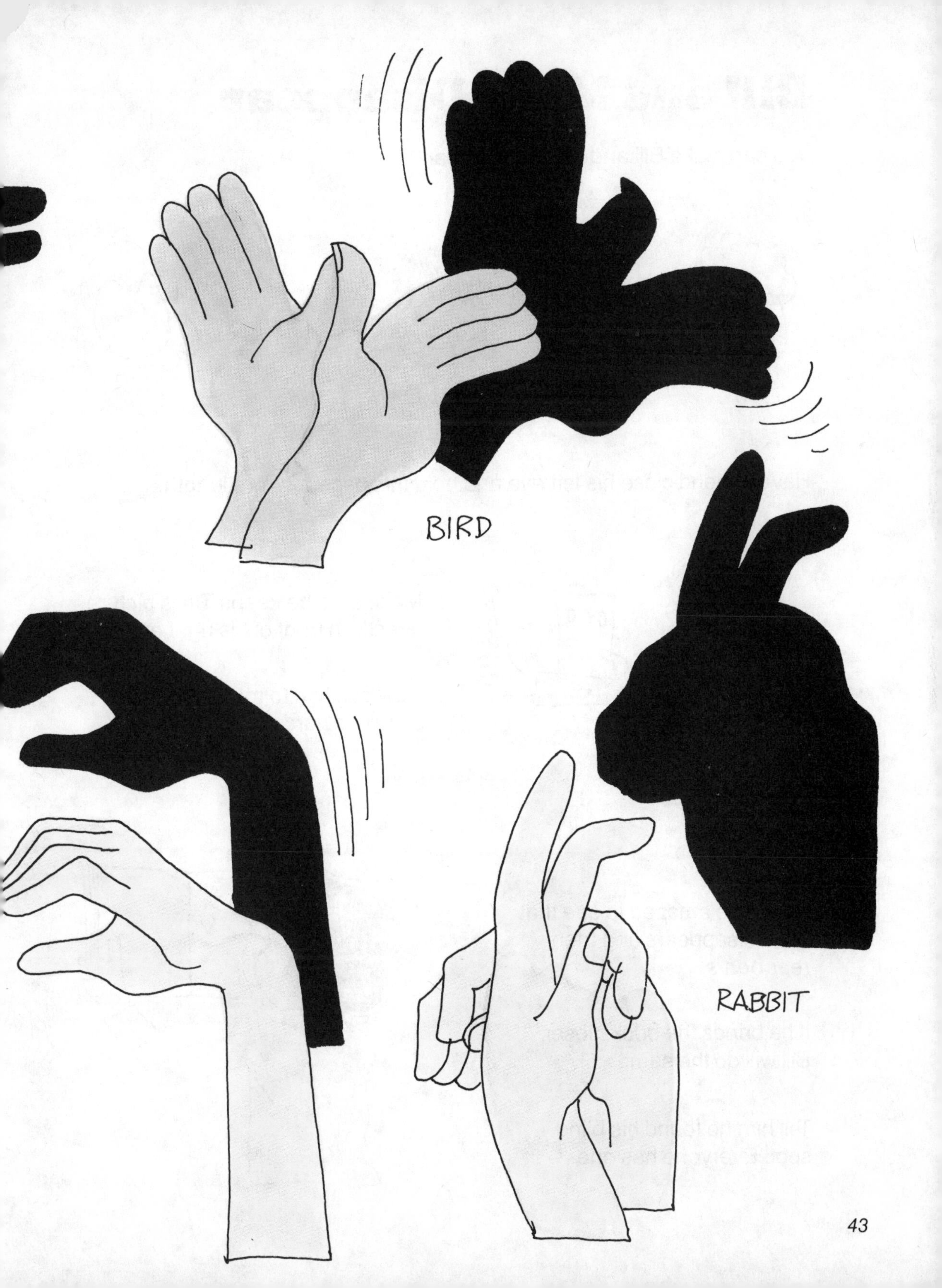
BIRD
RABBIT

Bill and Mary Disappear

You can make Bill and Mary disappear.

Have a friend close his left eye and hold this page at arm's length.

Make sure he keeps Tim's picture directly in front of his right eye!

Now ask him to move the page *slowly* toward his right eye.

He will be amazed to see that Mary disappears and then *reappears*.

If he brings the book closer, Bill will do the same.

Tell him he found his blind spot. Everyone has one.

Crazy Eyes

Here's some more tricks your eyes play on you.

Hold your fingers about one inch apart at arm's length. Stare at a distance beyond them. Do you see a *basketball?*

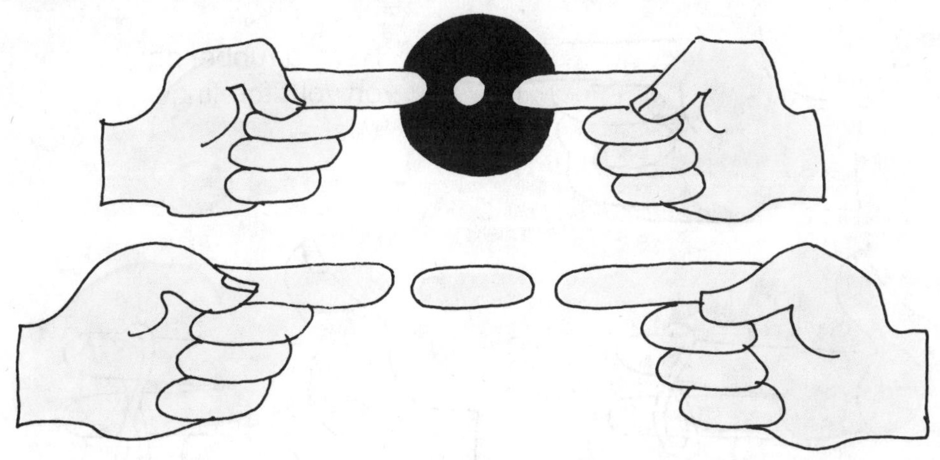

Move them closer to you and you'll see a *hot dog.*

If you put your fingers at a sharp angle you'll see a *heart.*

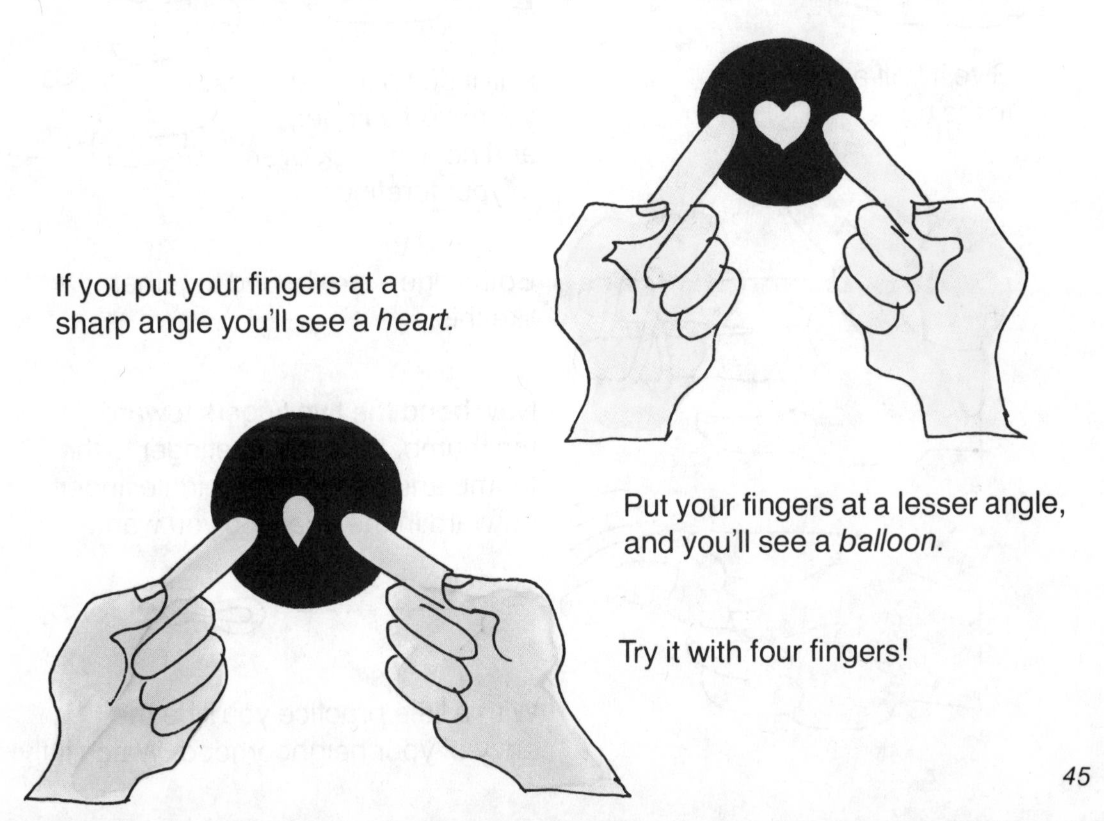

Put your fingers at a lesser angle, and you'll see a *balloon.*

Try it with four fingers!

Flies, Beware

Here's a great way to shoot down a fly at ten paces. All you need is a small, springy rubber band.

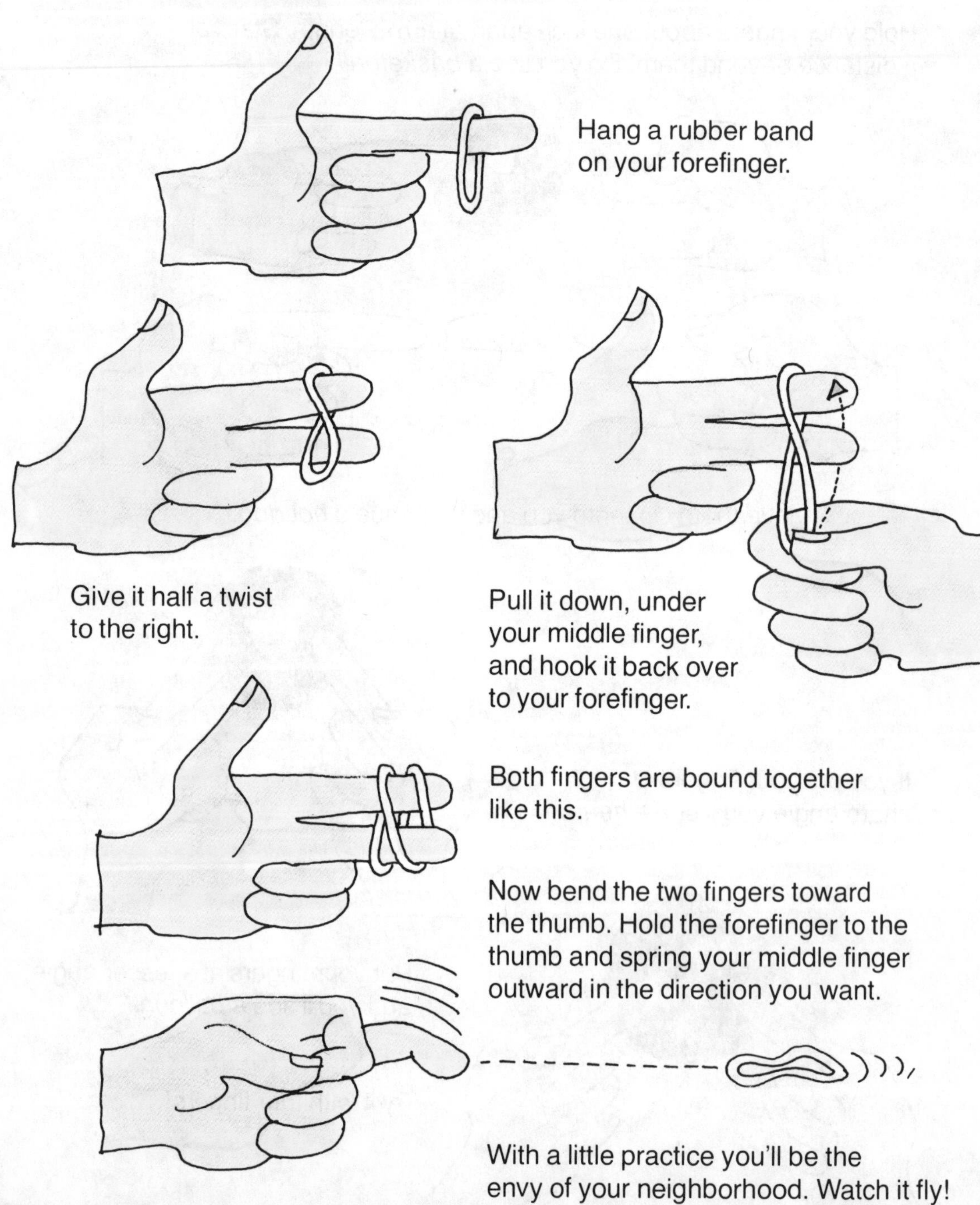

Hang a rubber band on your forefinger.

Give it half a twist to the right.

Pull it down, under your middle finger, and hook it back over to your forefinger.

Both fingers are bound together like this.

Now bend the two fingers toward the thumb. Hold the forefinger to the thumb and spring your middle finger outward in the direction you want.

With a little practice you'll be the envy of your neighborhood. Watch it fly!

Pulling Strings

Tie a piece of cord around a book.

Tie a string to the top of the cord and hang the book from a doorknob.

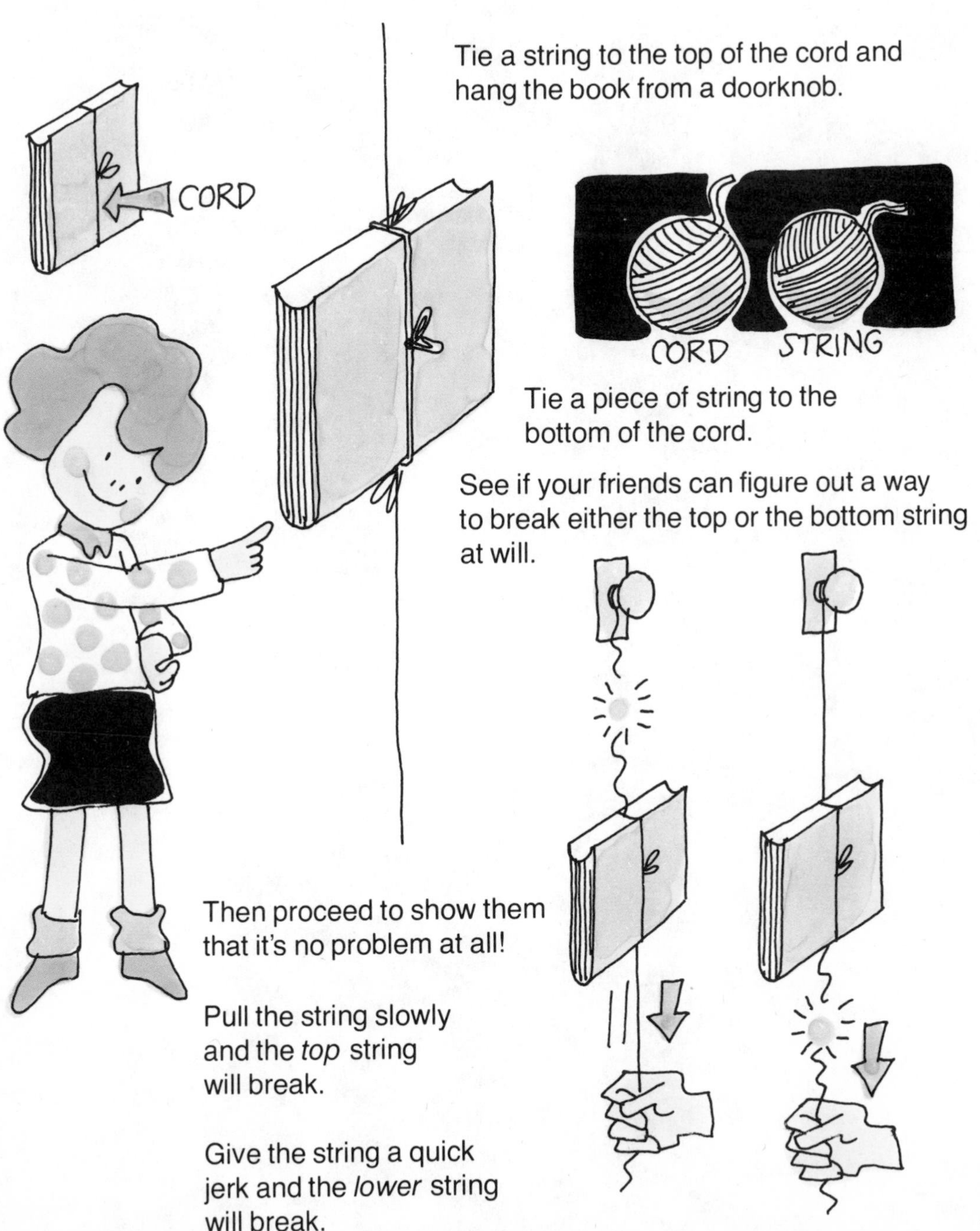

Tie a piece of string to the bottom of the cord.

See if your friends can figure out a way to break either the top or the bottom string at will.

Then proceed to show them that it's no problem at all!

Pull the string slowly and the *top* string will break.

Give the string a quick jerk and the *lower* string will break.